SIMPLE STRATEGIES FOR SUCCESSFUL VIRTUAL MEETINGS

SIMPLE STRATEGIES FOR **SUCCESSFUL** VIRTUAL MEETINGS

NATALIE SMITH

ISBN: 979-8-88640-054-0 (sc)
ISBN: 979-8-89031-891-6 (hc)
ISBN: 979-8-88640-056-4 (e)

Because of the dynamic nature of the Internet, any web addresses or links contained in this book may have changed since publication and may no longer be valid. The views expressed in this work are solely those of the author and do not necessarily reflect the views of the publisher, and the publisher hereby disclaims any responsibility for them.

THE EWINGS
PUBLISHING

One Galleria Blvd., Suite 1900, Metairie, LA 70001
(504) 702-6708

CONTENTS

We felt the effects of isolation during the pandemic. Let us build relationships and networks again. Let us find connections that improve team development. Virtual meetings give leaders the ability to do this in a more intimate and less intrusive way that will significantly impact office culture.

My name is Natalie Smith and I have been a team leader for more than two decades. I have led diverse teams in corporate America from novices to highly seasoned attorneys in a collaborative approach to maximize creativity, productivity, and team engagement. Before becoming a team leader, I created engaging activities for an office with over sixty employees. The activities started small from team lunches culminating in Super Bowl parties. Discussions of work and stress were disallowed. Employees were encouraged to fully engage in activities while building relationships with their fellow team members. The activities were simple and easy. We found that activities spanning generational pop cultures were very engaging for teams. I remember that our best activity was a seventies' luncheon wherein we fried spam and had jarred pig feet. At my last engagement activity with my first Fortune 500 company, we had every employee participating, including the managing partner of the firm.

People want to collaborate. People want to share activities. People love participating in group activities. Once you establish an engaging environment, you will increase employee buy-in and retention. Engaged teams have trust in their organization leading to exponential productivity and creativity. Except for employees seeking immediate leadership opportunities, I have **never** lost any employee I hired for any Fortune 500 Company. Even when an employee was disgruntled, my engagement activities and virtual management style kept employees productive, engaged and retained.

This book is designed to increase engagement on your team during virtual and in-person meetings. Starting a meeting with engagement activities ensures that your team members will have a strong link to you, their peers, and your organization. These activities will prompt your team to get to know one another, to learn about fellow employees' backgrounds and to facilitate the development of personal relationships. The activities are entertaining and may be used at the start of a meeting. However, to implement this new management style, you must first develop a personal relationship with each virtual team member. Because most teams no longer work in a brick-and-mortar building wherein you can say "hello" when you walk through the door or talk around a water cooler while seeing the wonderful pictures on your employees' desks, a leader must now explore their team's virtual workspaces.

This book is dedicated to:
My wonderful husband, Jeffery Smith

I would like to give personal thanks to my husband Jeffery Smith who has supported me for the past two decades as I navigated my tenure in corporate America. He is a leader in his own industry and provided me with great insight and activities to help me advance my career. Jeffery encouraged me to develop strong personal relationships with the people around me. Thank you, Jeffery, for being calm and patient and teaching me how to be calm and patient with my team. Thank you, Jeffery, for also giving me unqualified and unabridged trust. Being trusted also taught me how to trust others. Thank you, Jeffery, for being a compassionate teacher. By being a compassionate teacher, you taught me how to be a compassionate teacher for the people on my team. You taught me how to smile every day which helps me smile with those around me. You taught me how to be kind and how to love. And I try to be kind and teach those around me that I love them. You have been my best friend and best partner my entire life. I am so happy that you are in my life.

INTRODUCTION

C ongratulations on purchasing this book. After reading this book, you will become a better leader through building strong relationships on your virtual team. The activities in this book are five-minute activities that can be done in any group setting. The activities are fun and allow a leader to acquire background information on each team member. This book will additionally help leaders gain a better understanding of the employees on their team and in their organization. Because some employees no longer work in traditional brick-and-mortar offices, we do not have the opportunity to walk by and say "hello" to someone in their office or at their desk. Some employees can no longer see fellow employees' degrees/certificates/ diplomas posted on their walls, or family pictures they choose to have on their desk, or the artwork that they placed on their wall, or the books they read and kept on their bookshelf. Learning about the people you work with today requires different avenues post pandemic. This book will explore the routines we traditionally performed in pre-pandemic offices by translating them into a post pandemic management style.

Doing these activities on LinkedIn® increased my following weekly. I regularly receive feedback from people worldwide conveying their gratitude for my scavenger hunts, community service activities, and personal affirmations. I discovered that people want to connect. People do not want to be in a virtual world by themselves. They desire connections that are not work centered or management mandated. People want to collaborate by engaging in simple activities. I receive over four thousand views weekly on LinkedIn®. The peers on LinkedIn® volunteered with local charities and increased their engagement on their own teams.

This book explores my journey to lead virtual teams with positive engagement activities leading to increased productivity. To increase your teams' effectiveness within your division, establish strong partnerships with your customers and clients, and promote community activism within your organization, you first must build strong teams, even in this virtual, post pandemic environment. This book will teach you how to do just that.

Let this book inspire you to develop a virtual team in a positive manner. The activities are simple and enjoyable but have a tremendous impact on employee engagement and retention. Your employees and team members will be more creative and collaborative, eliminating physical separation and low morale. You will discover great ways to build a highly productive and motivated team from reading this book.

PART I

KNOWING YOUR TEAM MEMBERS

Pre-pandemic, we walked into an office and had the pleasure of meeting the people on our teams. We said, "good morning," shook hands, smiled, and physically interacted with the employees in our workspace. We went into employees' workspaces filled with pictures of significant others, children, family members, activities, and/or pets on their desks. Their walls displayed their diplomas and/or artwork. When people visited employees' workspaces, they could ask about the pictures on their desk, the diplomas on their walls, or the artwork displayed adjacent to those diplomas. When we met colleagues at the water cooler, we discussed popular TV shows, cooking recipes, or the latest news. We also shared meals in the break room or walked together in the parking lot for exercise. We learned about each other's home life, interests, and activities as well as purchased fundraiser items shared by our colleagues for their children or grandchildren placed in the break room.

The pandemic changed the way we interacted with each other. We no longer interacted in person but in a virtual environment. We could no longer walk into employees' offices and experience our peers' daily lives. However, the same activities we did in an office can be accomplished in a virtual environment. You can still get to know your team and develop relationships with them by being in their physical space, virtually. This book will teach you how to be in that same physical space with your team members in a virtual environment. It is important as a team leader, as well as a team member, to enter this virtual environment by first sharing your life and interests with your team. This will help your employees build connections and team comradery.

CHAPTER ONE

GET PERSONAL

Your Own Story

To build relationships in your team, you first must tell your own story. Telling that story is important because it builds bridges for the employees on your team and in your organization. Knowing your background will help your team members relate to you as well as to others on your team. Therefore, tell them about your history, where you are from, activities you enjoy, your family and educational background. A leader must share their personal story and interests with those on their team to help build stronger relationships. This first chapter is about you "getting personal." While we may shy away from being vulnerable or letting people into our private affairs, authentically sharing a part of yourself creates a unique bond with the listener.

During the first meeting with my manager in corporate America, the manager asked me about my husband and children, their ages, and the date I married. Every time I saw my manager, including almost thirty years later, the manager knew the names of my children and my husband. She asked about them, inquiring about their well-being. I happily talked about my children and my husband. I was shocked that she remembered their names but overly joyed that she had an interest in me personally.

As a leader, it starts with you sharing yourself so your team members feel comfortable sharing personal information with you. The very first step in this process is telling your own story from who you are, your educational background, your family and interests, your work history, as well as your work principles in an introductory meeting with your team. This should be done as soon as possible or in the first meeting after you adopt this virtual management style. By setting an example of sharing your background, you will allow each team member to get to know you and encourage them to share likewise. Even if you did not do this in your first virtual meeting, you can do this now and let your team know that you are starting this new virtual management style to build team rapport and engagement. The rapport begins with you candidly sharing personal information about your background. Be transparent with your team about your need to develop relationships with each team member. Honesty has always been a fundamental bedrock in a strong relationship.

On every new team, I allow my associates to get to know me. I tell them that I am from a rural town in South Georgia who grew up on the "wrong side of the tracks" in the watermelon capital of the world. And then I tell them that I spent my time on a farm roaming around barefoot as I collected eggs and fed the chickens. Most people laugh when they hear this. Laughter is a good sign that you are breaking through the awkwardness on your virtual team. This will give you a fantastic opportunity to develop greater rapport with your team. People love back stories and cannot wait to share their own. So be creative and start telling your story in an imaginative way that engages the listener and hopefully garners laughter on your team. If you are not funny, give them the facts and they will still be equally impressed with your vulnerability, openness, and candid style. It is not the laughter that is important but the meaningful connection with your team.

I also share funny stories about my family. I love to share stories about how my grandmother tried to kill me by making me kill snakes on our farm while she hid inside the house at a distance. Yes... these are true stories and happened on several occasions. The best story with my grandmother is her sending me on a screened porch with a hoe to kill a snake. As soon as she pushed me onto the porch, she shut the door and locked it. At this time, I was a middle schooler. I raised the hoe, closed my eyes, swung down, and obviously missed the snake because my eyes were closed. The snake slid off the porch through the screened door, turned around and tried to bite me several times. Because the snake was rising to bite me, (snakes strike by lurching their body forward and upward), the snake hit the screened porch door. During this entire time, my grandmother never unlocked the door.

If you have exciting stories from your childhood, share them with your team. If you do not have exciting stories, share different activities and hobbies that you engaged in as a child. Start the story from the beginning, sharing your incredible background and laying the foundation for great relationships.

Then tell them about your educational background and work history. Your team needs to know your full background to help them know about your talent and what you bring to the team.

Lastly, a leader must share their ethics and values, clearly stating their expectations for work quality, training, and team engagement. Your team needs to know that competency is valued, but grace is extended always. Let your team know that you value etiquette, accessibility, and collaboration. Your team needs to know that you are available and will compassionately reach out immediately when opportunities arise. I created a team chat and encouraged employees to log in every morning to say "good morning" to the entire team. The team could write anything and post any picture in the team chat. Other employees would comment on posts and pictures shared in the team chat. The team chat became our virtual "water cooler."

Employees often said, "good morning" when they walked into a traditional office. Equally, leaders often exchanged pleasantries with their employees in traditional brick-and-mortar workspaces. This social norm should not be eliminated because we are in a virtual environment. Leaders should respond daily in daily chats with their virtual teams. Moreover, leaders should create virtual office hours where employees can "drop in" to discuss any topic or problem-solve with their leader. Likewise, leaders should begin every communication, whether through instant message (IM), chats, emails, texts, or calls with pleasantries. A leader must consistently show their values in all communications.

Your Pictures and Walls

This chapter will discuss the importance of sharing your pictures from your desk and on your wall with your virtual team. This will further help your team get to know you.

If you had a traditional office, what pictures would you place on your desk? This requires some thought. You may have had to pack up your old office or workspace during the pandemic and take home your personal items. Pull those pictures out and now share them with your team in a virtual environment. The things you held most dear were more likely on your desk. However, this activity gives you the opportunity to exchange the pictures you had in your traditional office or workspace for pictures that truly motivate you. Other people will have insight into your favorite people, activities, and/or pets. Be creative! Find or print your favorite pictures, put them in frames, and share them with your team. You do not have to do this activity in one setting. This activity may occur over several virtual meetings. You could entitle this five-minute engagement activity "Get to Know You."

Take time to do this activity over a few virtual meetings. Setting an amount of time dedicated to this activity gives employees more certainty but refrain from interrupting natural conversations flowing from this exercise. For those employees who are interested, they will be more receptive to learning about you. Then, you will need to shift this activity over to each employee, giving them the same amount of time over the same number of virtual meetings to share their pictures, family members, and/or pets.

Keep your commentary low. Give your employees the facts to let them form their own opinions and conclusions about you. Do not try to influence your audience. Your spouse or significant partner, children, or activities are what they are. Share it with your team and give a little history about the picture. You can explain where the picture was taken, who was in the picture, the date the picture was taken, and the role that person, pet or activity plays in your life.

Try not to overwhelm your audience with more than three or four pictures, the number of pictures most people have in their traditional office. Select wisely so that you can authentically share a part of you that is vulnerable and personal, opening the door to a personal relationship as opposed to just a professional one.

CHAPTER SUMMARY/KEY TAKEAWAYS

In summary, being authentic and vulnerable about your background while asking the same from the people on your team is the first step in creating a successful virtual environment. Sharing really is caring when you are dealing with a virtual team. What you start in your team environment will expand to various parts of your organization and business partnerships. Learning to be personable in a team environment indeed highlights the importance of being personable in business dealings and relationships. This will strengthen and create strong business alliances within your team and for your team. You can do these initial steps by:

- sharing your personal information about school, family, pets, educational background, art, and/or favorite activities.

- asking your employees to share information about their school, family, pets, educational background, art, and/or favorite activities.

- collecting baby pictures and creating a game wherein your team matches the pictures with their fellow employees. You may also collect baby pictures of your employees' partners and/or children and ask your team to match the picture to a fellow employee.

- creating bingo cards with different activities learned about your employees' backgrounds and asking each team member to match their fellow employee to a different activity. The employees may then submit the card for a prize for most correct answers.

In the next chapter, we will discuss fun and engaging activities that can further build a strong relationship with the people on your team. Not only will the leader have strong relationships with their team, but also the team members will have strong relationships with each other. As indicated in the last two bullet points, team engagement starts with first learning about each other in a creative way. You can create games that help employees know about one another. The next chapter will focus on deepening our understanding of each employee by engaging in activities that are fun, free, and easy to do in a virtual or in-person environment.

CHAPTER TWO

VIRTUAL OFFICES

S haring your personal story is essential in a virtual environment. The more you share about yourself, the better the personal relationship is with your team members. You may initially share the information from the previous chapter in a group environment. Relationships, however, are formed in one-on-one interactions.

One on One

It is important for you to develop a personal relationship with each person on your team. To do that, you must obtain the same information you shared about yourself from each team member in a personal setting. You may have this first one-on-one meeting either virtually or in-person. The purpose of the meeting should not be centered on work but focused on building a relationship with that employee. A leader should set up a one-on-one meeting with each team member. If you have a budget for the same, you could do this first meeting over a virtual luncheon wherein you send your employee lunch or allow them to purchase lunch on their corporate credit card. While you are getting to know that employee, you will be sharing a meal as if you were in a break room. This is a great way to get to know your team members. Be an active listener, listening more than talking. Be complimentary.

Be compassionate. Be patient. Allow your employee to set the pace of this meeting. You can start the meeting by asking questions to prompt your employee to share.

Also, be observant. If the meeting is virtual, positively comment on the employee's surroundings or choice of virtual screen backgrounds. As a leader, you must develop great people skills that encourage connections. Then, set recurring monthly one-on-one meetings with each team member to continue to develop your personal relationship as well as manage work productivity.

Please remember that getting to know your team is not a memory test. The benefit of being in a virtual environment allows you a pencil and sheet of paper where you can write information down and save it into a file for each employee. Ask the employee about their prior work history and significant dates in their life, i.e., birth, work anniversary, marriage, etc. Print the names and ages of any children, their children's schools and activities, the names of their partners, their partner's occupation, the breed and name of their pets, the region in which they live, etc. It is important that you ask about their children and their well-being at the beginning of each one-on-one meeting. It is important that you ask about their spouses/partners, vacations, and activities at the beginning of each one-on-one meeting. It is also important that you ask about family activities, pets, or weekend projects at the beginning of each one-on-one meeting. The more you know about each individual employee will help you better manage that employee.

Team leaders often make the mistake of objectifying relationships in a team environment. Each team member must be managed subjectively, based on who they are, what they know, and the skill level they possess at that time. Freely communicate with your team members during the one-on-one meetings so that you learn more about each individual team member.

Team Environment

After you get to know each team member personally, you now must build a collaborative team environment. This means that each team member must become vulnerable in a group setting so that you can build the foundations for a strong team that will better serve your clients, customers, and partners. In the first chapter, we discussed creating games and activities with people sharing their family stories/dynamics/histories, interests, and/or pets. Spending a few minutes before each meeting to do this does not detract from your work productivity but strengthens it. Accordingly, make sure you begin each meeting with water cooler moments and share outs. Recognize birthdays, work anniversaries, marriage anniversaries, and work-related achievements. Have employees share out successful work activities, obtaining employee participation in the meeting. Allow employees to talk about the water cooler moments, i.e., a popular TV show, a favorite cooking recipe, weekend activities, etc.

Additionally, have a pre-arranged time for each associate to share about themselves in a five-minute format, sharing background information about their family, activities, hobbies, and/or pets. Memorialize any information you learn about an employee in their file and use this information when you connect with that employee. Also, follow up with an employee on information that is sensitive to the employee, i.e., sick child, vacation, anniversary, difficult work project, etc. The employee will appreciate a leader that remembers personal and work-related activities in the employee's life.

During virtual meetings, be observant when spouses, children or pets appear on your employee's screen. Some people may have their pets in their lap or right next to them during a virtual meeting. Ask questions about the pet and invite that employee to share information about their pet. You may also see employee's spouses or children during virtual meetings. Ask to speak with the spouse or child, if appropriate. Make sure to compliment the employee while talking with the spouse or child if they appear on camera.

Team meetings are best served by the interests of the team members. While you may not get to everything on your agenda, it is more important that you develop a strong relationship with each employee so that you can increase productivity, engagement, and partnership. Most leaders want to jump right into business. As a leader, you must set the tone for meetings and create warm, safe spaces for team members to congregate and share ideas.

I recently had a meeting with a divisional chair in a different department about a matter for which she needed my assistance. Before beginning the meeting, however, I asked about her virtual screen background, where she was located, and any other information she brought up during that conversation. The associate smiled and was happy to share that she was married, that her adult children had left home, and the activities she and her spouse engaged in the previous evening. Once we first established a relationship, we then could discuss business. That divisional manager then "liked" my posts on LinkedIn®. We had developed a personal relationship that underscored the business relationship.

I advise employees, business partners, as well as other divisional leaders, that we cannot discuss business without getting to know each other.

I have had more positive feedback from my business partners than my own teams. Every partnership has been fruitful and led to greater partnerships. Thus, it is important to get to know the people you are working with and develop a friendship before you discuss business. A great way to think of this is "people before business." If you use this motto in every interaction, you will have a successful relationship with the people on your team as well as your business partners.

Safe Environments

Virtual team meetings should be safe environments for all team members. In today's social media obsession, some people have relaxed social etiquette in favor of destructive manners and communications. Consistently showing your ethics and values, however, will allow you to fairly and immediately address opportunities with these employees through one-on-one coaching and feedback sessions as well as remedial measures during virtual team meetings. Hence, do not delay in addressing issues that do not meet your expectations in a virtual environment. Address matters timely and privately, initially, showing compassion. Patiently listen for ways to positively resolve conflict. Not addressing an issue timely, however, will erode team confidence and undermine a collaborative team environment. Nevertheless, a leader can immediately address and implement changes in a virtual environment by candidly addressing the opportunities deteriorating team engagement and morale. It is never too late to improve office culture in a virtual environment as this new virtual environment is a byproduct of the pandemic and unfortunately colored by some people's crass behavior on social media. Honestly discussing the need to create a safe and positive environment for every employee is crucial and necessary. Failure to correctly halt behaviors that lower morale on a virtual team may lead to disengagement. Be forthcoming with your team and redirect negative behavior with positive messages modifying unwelcomed behaviors.

Your team needs to know that you will be a trusted partner in this virtual environment. You build this trust through developing personal relationships with each team member and protecting your employees in the virtual environment. Building trust is a key component to successfully managing your team. Being consistent with your ethics and values will help you build a trusting, personal relationship with each team member.

CHAPTER SUMMARY/KEY TAKEAWAYS

This concludes the information contained in this chapter on building personal relationships and positive, virtual team meetings. The information contained within this section will help you build a strong foundation for your team as well as your business partners. You can use the strategies in this section to create five-minute engagement activities utilized at the start of team meetings.

We will now focus on activities you can do to further build that personal relationship between you and each team member and then your team members and the entire office for a collaborative virtual office. In the next section of the book, I will give you different scavenger hunts that you can use with your team to build engagement. I have used several virtual activities to build strong team environments. My most successful virtual activity, however, has been virtual scavenger hunts. My scavenger hunts have been utilized globally to help people feel connected. The activities are free and usually involve items that are easily found within a person's home. Scavenger hunts do not take significant time and are a great way to increase positive engagement on your team while bringing people together.

PART II

VIRTUAL
SCAVENGER HUNTS

As a leader, I have tried several virtual activities to build team engagement and business partnerships. My most successful virtual activity, however, has been virtual scavenger hunts. Indeed, I lead a virtual scavenger hunt on Mondays on LinkedIn® which is viewed several thousand times around the world. I am amazed at the feedback I receive from people in other countries that follow these scavenger hunts. The scavenger hunts are simple and take no more than five minutes. The activities always involve items that are in people's homes. In this section, I will share with you some very successful scavenger hunts that I have implemented over the last three years, post pandemic.

CHAPTER THREE

SCAVENGER HUNTS AROUND YOUR DESK

S cavenger hunts can be utilized in any meeting and are highly effective in a virtual meeting. Most remote employees have home offices or workspaces where they work daily. The scavenger hunt gives you an opportunity to be physically present in a remote employee's workspace the same as if you walked into their office or workspace in a traditional brick-and-mortar building. The difference is most people will not display their pictures, diplomas and/or artwork in a remote workspace or home office. However, there are certain things that people keep in their remote workspace or home office similar to what they kept in a traditional brick-and-mortar building. Focusing on these things usually increases employee participation and will create team connections and comradery during a virtual meeting.

Desk Scavenger Hunt Activities

Scavenger hunts are simple to do if you focus on common items people have in their workspace. Below, I will list ideas on simple scavenger hunts you can use during your virtual meetings:

1. The easiest activity for a scavenger hunt in a remote employee's work environment is to focus on the equipment provided by the company. Have each employee take a picture of their workspace and share it in chat during the virtual meeting. The activity helps develop your employees' competencies with technology by upskilling each employee's ability to upload images from different platforms into the virtual meeting.

2. Another scavenger hunt idea for remote workers is to ask each employee to take a picture with a writing instrument and post it in chat. With this activity, you can focus on how many employees have the same type of writing instrument, i.e., pencils, blue ink pens, black ink pens, etc. If you have someone that has a unique writing instrument, like a red ink pen, highlight that for the team. You can also count how many similar writing instruments employees have on your team, i.e., 80% have black ink pens. This activity highlights individuality as well as group commonalities. If an employee has a pencil that has bite marks, ask that employee to tell you what happened to their pencil. The activity is fun and simple. The activity also develops your employees' competencies with technology.

3. Another scavenger hunt idea for remote workers is each employee taking a picture of paper at or near the employee's desk and uploading the same to the chat section of the virtual meeting. With this activity, the leader may focus on how many employees have loose leaf paper, tablets, pads, index cards, etc. You can repeat the same questions from the previous scavenger hunt suggestion. The leader should look for similarities and differences and highlight them for their team.

4. Another scavenger hunt idea for remote workers is taking a picture of a cup, glass, mug, water bottle, etc. at or near the employee's desk and uploading the same to the chat section of the virtual meeting. Again, this activity should have the leader asking about similarities and differences on the team. With this activity, additionally, you can ask each employee to describe what beverages they drink while working. Tell your team to keep it clean and not discuss alcoholic beverages consumed during working hours to make them laugh. Find the similarities and differences in the types of drinks consumed by your team. Find out if employees are coffee or tea drinkers. Find out who on your team does not like coffee or tea. This question can lead to a lot of information about your team as well as help you plan your next in-person outing. These questions also lead to an engaging environment, further building strong relationships on your team.

5. Another scavenger hunt idea is having each employee take a picture of snacks/food at their desk and uploading the image to the chat feature of the virtual meeting. Use the information from the previous scavenger hunts to find out more information about the similarities and differences on your team. This will also help you find out about the eating habits of your team members. Some team members may be vegan or vegetarian. This is a great way to learn more about your team members and help you plan your next in-person outing.

These scavenger hunts are just a few ideas to get you started on learning about your employees' workspaces. To build the greatest engagement, I have kept this list limited to merely five activities. As your employees become more engaged, ask your employees to create the next activity for team building. Getting your employees involved is also a way to create and maintain team engagement in a virtual environment. Have fun and be collaborative! Allow your employees to develop their own ideas as you engage in a virtual scavenger hunt around the employees' remote workspaces or offices.

CHAPTER SUMMARY/KEY TAKEAWAYS

This section will help your employees learn about their fellow employees' workspaces. These activities will give you the opportunity to physically observe each remote employee's workspace similar to being present in that employee's traditional brick-and-mortar office and workspace. As a leader, you will have an opportunity to observe things that are important to your employees and develop a deeper personal relationship with each employee.

In the next chapter, we will broaden the scope of our scavenger hunt to items in your employees' homes. These scavenger hunts will not be intrusive but will focus on items kept in people's homes that bring a sense of comradery to your team.

CHAPTER FOUR

SCAVENGER HUNTS AROUND YOUR HOME

After completing scavenger hunts around a remote employee's workspace, creating scavenger hunts throughout your employees' homes is another way to build strong relationships on your team. The activities usually center around items found in a person's home.

Home Scavenger Hunt Activities

I have used many activities to build team engagement. I initially used fun facts and inter-team competitions to build team engagement. Home scavenger hunts, however, are simple to do if you focus on common things people have in their homes. Some scavenger hunt activities below have been viewed worldwide on my LinkedIn® account and have been extraordinarily successful. These activities should be a launchpad for greater team engagement. The list below contains ideas on simple scavenger hunts you can use during your virtual meetings:

- It's scavenger hunt Monday on the last Monday in October! Wear a costume to a meeting without telling anyone you are in costume! See who looks at you strangely!

- It's scavenger hunt Monday! Find a blue jean jacket! Remember, you used to wear it all the time! Tell your team about some blue jean jacket memories…PG rated of course!

- It's scavenger hunt Monday! Find something that you didn't do your best job on! Don't give up! Try again! You can start over!

- Its scavenger hunt Monday on 9/11. As we remember those patriots killed during this attack, let's find something in our homes that helps us recognize that we rallied together on 9/12. Share with your team and remember that not only does our job holds us together but also our privileged citizenship as Americans!

- It's scavenger hunt Monday! Find a magnifying glass this Labor Day and see what's lurking in your grill before you fire it up! Do your best Sherlock Holmes' impression! I feel for you if you don't know who I'm talking about. Take pictures and share with your team on Tuesday!

- It's scavenger hunt Monday! Today is free play. Find something in your home that holds special meaning and share it with your team. Be open about why you picked what you picked! Your team will love it! My pick is a family shot with my entire family taken by my next-door neighbor who is a professional photographer! I am so very happy and blessed to have such wonderful, caring, beautiful, and loving people in my life!

- It's scavenger hunt Monday! Find a few of "My Favorite Things" and share with your team!

- It's scavenger hunt Monday! Find a boom box! You read it correctly! Put it on your shoulder and share the image with your team! Get ready to laugh with your peers!

- It's scavenger hunt Monday! Find a play bill or picture from the theater! Isn't my daughter cute? See what shows your peers have attended, or performed in, or watched their children perform in! High school plays count too! Tell the tales of your theater life with your team!

- It's scavenger hunt Monday! Take a picture with your favorite sleuth from a mystery show! A great team can solve any mystery…for every real problem, there is a real solution… so be a team player and trust all the characters on your team!

- It's scavenger hunt Monday! Take a picture in your favorite socks and share with your team! You know you received some crazy socks as a gift! Tell the tale!

- It's scavenger hunt Monday! Take a picture in a shower cap! Again, keep it clean and share it with your team!

- It's scavenger hunt Monday! Take a picture in your favorite chair! Don't tell the other chairs and share with your team! Let them know if you ever fell asleep in it!

- It's scavenger hunt Monday! Take a picture holding a silver dollar! Where did you find it? Tell the tale and share it with your team!

- It's scavenger hunt Monday! Take a picture with your junk drawer! Don't try to clean it up! Haha! Let everyone on your team know where you hide things and why the drawer is full of take-out menus!

- It's scavenger hunt Monday! Take a picture of a game you play that is really for kids. Haha. Your team is starting to know you and are not surprised!

- It's scavenger hunt Monday! Take a picture of yourself before you style your hair! What? I'm not ashamed! Your team needs to see the real you! And no, I am not with my granddaughter now!

These scavenger hunts are just a few ideas to get you started on learning about your employees' home lives. I have kept this list condensed as I do scavenger hunts weekly. To build the greatest engagement, ask your employees to create the next scavenger hunt activity. Getting your employees involved is also a way to create and maintain team engagement in a virtual environment. Have fun and be collaborative! Allow employees to develop their own activities as you engage in a virtual scavenger hunt around the home.

EPILOGUE/CONCLUSION

It is easy to bring an employee's lifestyle in a traditional brick-and-mortar building to a virtual environment. Being in a virtual environment should not change the way you engage with employees. Creating that same environment in a virtual format will strengthen your team, create greater engagement, increase productivity, and help employee retention. Whether you are the leader or a team member, our pre-pandemic work environment must translate seamlessly into the post pandemic world we live in. Teams are either 100% virtual or hybrid. These strategies will work in person as well as virtually. Because some employees no longer have traditional brick-and-mortar offices or workspaces, we must create a warm, virtual environment that welcomes our employees, visitors, peers, and business partners. Following the principles outlined in this book will help you create exceptional team engagement leading to increased productivity and employee retention as well as exceptional customer service for your business partners.

BIBLIOGRAPHY

The content of this book is based on the author's 20+ year leadership style and corporate America tenure. The author did not rely on any written materials published through books or online articles but developed these strategies and principles during her management.

ACKNOWLEDGMENTS

There were many key people who inspired me throughout the process of authoring this book. First, again, I acknowledge my husband, Jeffery Smith, who inspired me for the past two decades on leadership principles for successfully managing my teams. I also acknowledge Alycia Anderson who was a sounding board for solid leadership principles as I managed my teams these past five years. Her insight and wisdom were invaluable in helping me manage my team in an objective manner. I would also like to acknowledge my long-term college friend, Rose Calloway, for providing guidance and objectivity with team management issues as they arose these past few months.

ABOUT THE AUTHOR

Natalie Smith is an experienced Managing Attorney of a virtual staff counsel office for a Fortune 500 company handling insurance defense and commercial litigation. Prior to her current position, she assumed the helm of another Fortune 500 insurance company's in-house staff counselling firm in 2015 with five attorneys. At her departure, the office was virtual and had ten attorneys and a junior Managing Attorney. Prior to this position, Natalie successfully led a team for another Fortune 500 company, training attorneys and insurance professionals for more than 17 years. Having practiced law in leadership roles for more than two decades, she has a wealth of experience in the insurance industry with measurable and objective results in virtual leadership, litigation and firm management from working with three Fortune 500 insurance carriers and litigating more than 2000 cases of varying degrees of complexity, including complex litigation, wrongful death claims and appeals. Natalie has successfully handled more than 1000 depositions, tried more than 55 cases, and participated in more than 150 mediations. Moreover, Natalie has experience in negotiating and litigating all aspects of personal injury cases, as well as an array of civil and commercial litigation.

Natalie has strong leadership skills and experiences with virtual branding and performance management. She successfully developed metrics, analytics, and objective measurements to create, improve and streamline work processes and efficiencies while building team engagement and trust. Natalie developed core principles for a successful team. She is likewise skilled in Management, Coaching, Strategy and Business Development. She has been an invaluable asset to her firms with practical and simple team strategies that produced extraordinary team productivity and business partnerships. Every carrier has adopted her processes nationally.

Natalie offers her experience as a consultant to help teams build successful relationships and increase their productivity in a virtual environment.

Natalie is available to help you develop simple strategies to build a successful team through her consulting firm, Simple Strategies Consultants, LLC. She may be contacted at nataliesmith@simple strategiesconsultants.com.

Printed in the USA
CPSIA information can be obtained
at www.ICGtesting.com
LVHW041945020224
770736LV00002BA/49